D0966441

Pure ♥ Cute

Pure ♥ Cute

Beverly West and Jason Bergund

**Andrews McMeel
Publishing, LLC**

Kansas City • Sydney • London

09 10 11 12 13 TEN 10 9 8 7 6 5 4 3 2

ISBN-13: 978-0-7407-7403-4
ISBN-10: 0-7407-7403-4

Library of Congress Control Number: 2009925647

www.andrewsmcmeel.com

Attention: Schools and Businesses
Andrews McMeel books are available at quantity discounts with bulk purchase for educational, business, or sales promotional use. For information, please write to: Special Sales Department, Andrews McMeel Publishing, LLC, 1130 Walnut Street, Kansas City, Missouri 64106.

Introduction

Pure Cute has existed from the very beginning of time. Throughout history, it has been cuddled, coddled, hugged, held, embraced, and petted. It has been sought after and adopted, lost and found, put in pet shop windows and sold for a fortune. Now, for the first time in history, all the faces, tails, paws, and soft pink noses of *Pure Cute* come together in this uplifting album of incredibly adorable photos and revelations that will be life transforming for all who cuddle up with it.

In this book you'll learn how to put *Pure Cute* to work in every arena of your life—love, money, health, and happiness—and you'll begin to understand the miraculous, untapped power of the cuteness that is all around you. It can increase your own cute quotient and bring a greater sense of joy and well-being to each and every moment of your life.

Pure Cute is every cuddly kitten and every adorable pup, bunny, colt, or cub you have imagined . . . and is beyond your sweetest dreams.

Pure ♥ Cute

Waking Up/
Awareness

Right now, with the knowledge of
Pure Cute, you are waking up from a
deep sleep and becoming aware:
aware of the knowledge, aware of the
cute, and aware that puppies are most
adorable when they're together.

Abundance

It is up to each person to summon their vision of abundance. So take a moment today to ask yourself what you really want: the puppy on the right, the puppy on the left, or both?

Safety/Security

To feel safe is to know the
power of cute and to realize
that when you are this adorable,
no one is going to push you
out of the nest.

Independence

At the beginning of a new journey,
remember that even though you
may be leaving the nest,
you'll always be one of the litter.

The Power of
Letting Go

Don't think that you are caught in
the grip of something larger than yourself.
Rather, consider that you are just
being carried to a better place.

Finding Your Voice

Express yourself.
You'll feel cuter once you do.

Guilt

There are good feelings and bad feelings, and you know the difference. One makes you feel good, and the other gets you gated in the kitchen for the rest of the day. It's treatlessness, it's guilt, and it's that wet spot on the new carpet. Now is the time to summon your cute. Once you do, no matter how big the mess, everybody will eventually forgive you.

The Size of Beauty

Always be on the lookout for the cute. But you have to look closely, because although sometimes cute is very big, other times it is very, very small.

Expectation

Expectation is a powerful force,
because it draws what you desire
into your life. Think this is a lie?
Just take a look at Kermit here.
Wouldn't you give him a treat?

Rest/
Relaxation

Sometimes, it's only when we are
lying still and in the silence that we realize
that cute is in progress.

Appetite

Indulge yourself. Cute has no calories.

Reliance

Lean on the cute.

Meditation

Think cute thoughts.

Opportunity

When cuteness speaks,
listen.
That's all you have to do.

Harmony/
Cooperation

No matter who you are
or where you're going,
someone has used their special talent
to help you get there.

From Both Sides
Now

Sometimes,
if you think out of the basket,
things get even cuter.

Dreams/Sleep

The forces of cute are still operating
when we're asleep.

Sharing

Cuteness is contagious.

Friendship

Life is much cuter

when you've got friends.

Facing Facts

When you look life in the face,
you will often discover
that things are a lot cuter
than you thought they were.

Diversity

Cute is color-blind.

Partnership

We are cute together.
Not as controllers
but as a living, purring process.

Family/
Togetherness

Just like family and togetherness, cuteness is a sunbeam shining through the storm clouds of life.

Standing Out

Don't be afraid to make a statement.

Cuteness is always in style.

Alone Time

In those precious few moments
when we are able to just be by ourselves
and do nothing, cuteness happens.

Humor

Don't suppress the cute.
It can be more satisfying than
honor or dignity.

Faith

When you are experiencing a crisis
of faith and searching for evidence
of a loving higher power,
just look into the eyes of a puppy.

Reaching for the
Stars

While you're pursuing your possibilities, keep your thoughts constantly focused on your personal peak. Just make sure you don't get so far ahead of yourself that you sprain your cute muscle.

Learning to Fly

Don't be afraid to try your wings
and learn new things.
Clumsy can be cute.

Baggage

Just remember,
when you open up the suitcase,
amazing new and cute possibilities
jump in.

Companionship

Two is cuter than one.

Exhaustion

Cute rejuvenation

works from the ground up.

Curiosity

Curiosity never killed the cute.

Magic

When you are one with the cute,
miracles happen.

Contentment

Be here now.

Cuteness happens in the moment.

Big Dreams

Remember, sometimes the cutest things come in small packages.

Similarities and Differences

Cute is the great equalizer.

No Limits

You can never have
too much cuteness.

Cheer Up

Lovebirds are cute,
even though they are blue.

Photo Credits